Science Close-Up
ROCKS

Written by Lin Bass
Illustrated by James Spence

A GOLDEN BOOK • NEW YORK
Western Publishing Company, Inc., Racine, Wisconsin 53404

© 1991 Western Publishing Company, Inc. Illustrations © 1991 James Spence. All rights reserved.
Printed in the U.S.A. No part of this book may be reproduced or copied in any form without
written permission of the publisher. All trademarks are the property of Western Publishing
Company, Inc. Library of Congress Catalog Card Number: 91-72261 ISBN: 0-307-12852-0

The Earth Is Made of Rocks!

Rocks are everywhere. Very small rocks are called **pebbles**.
Medium-sized rocks are called **stones**. When they are very big,
they are called **boulders**. And there is the planet Earth. It is
one giant rock!

Mountain climbers go up and down sky-high mounds of rock.
Deep-sea divers walk on ocean floors of rock. Desert travelers
walk and ride on tiny, sun-baked grains of rock.

When you stroll along a beach, each step you take is on thousands of grains of sand, each of which was worn away from a larger rock. When you make a mud pie, you are using small bits of rock. There are rocks in city sidewalks and city parks, on country roads, on farmland, on sheep ranches. We live in a world of rocks.

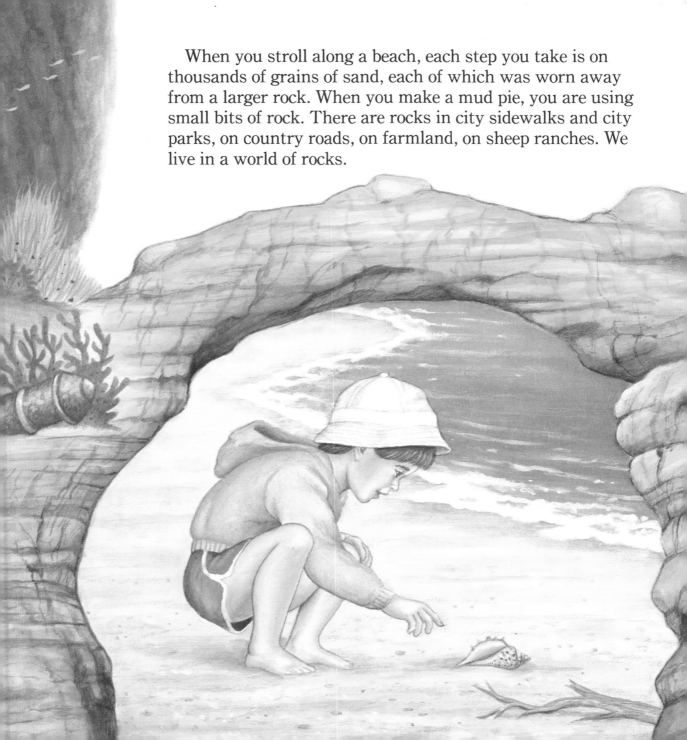

Over millions of years, mountains are worn down by erosion.

Are Mountains Forever?

When you look at a mountain, it is hard to imagine that it will not last forever. But even as you look, the mountain may be getting smaller. Bit by bit, it is being worn away by wind, storms, rivers, and other forces of nature. This wearing away is called *erosion*. Over millions of years, erosion makes mountains into molehills.

While some mountains are shrinking, others are being built. One way a mountain comes into being is by *eruption*. A powerful force inside the earth cracks open the ground and drives a huge mass of rock up, up, up...until it is a mountain.

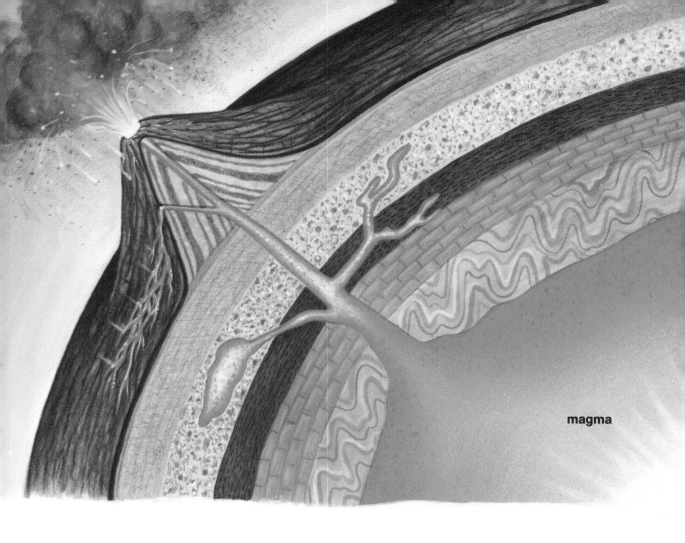

magma

All of the world's rocks are part of our planet's solid outer layer. This layer is called the earth's *crust*. The crust may be no more than six miles deep—or a lot deeper. But no matter how thick it is, just below the earth's crust is a kind of rock that is so hot, it is in liquid form. It is called *magma*. If you have seen pictures of a volcano erupting, you have seen magma. When magma is pushed through the earth's crust, it is called *lava*.

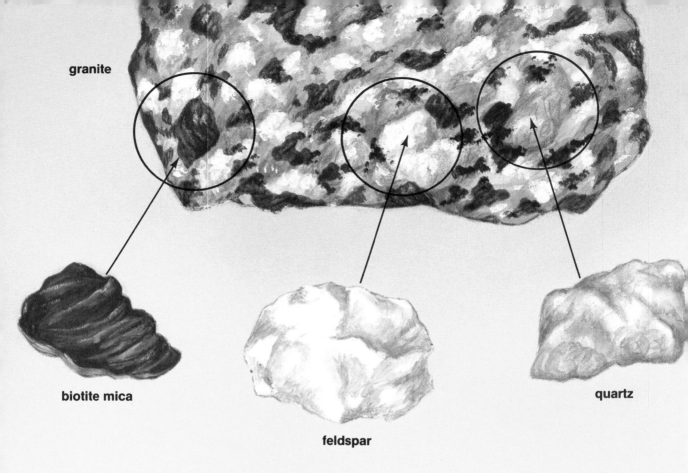

granite

biotite mica

feldspar

quartz

What Are Rocks Made Of?

Rocks are made up of one or more *minerals*. A mineral is a natural chemical substance that is not a plant or an animal. Each mineral is a solid. It may be made up of single elements, such as carbon, calcium, copper, and so forth, or of combinations of elements forming compounds. Bits of these minerals are what rocks are composed of, the way blades of grass make up a lawn.

rock salt

chlorite schist

lapis lazuli

Rocks can vary in color from light to dark, depending on the kind of minerals they contain. If these minerals are hard, the rock is hard. If the minerals are soft, the rock is soft. If the minerals are heavy, the rock is heavy. If the minerals are light, the rock is light.

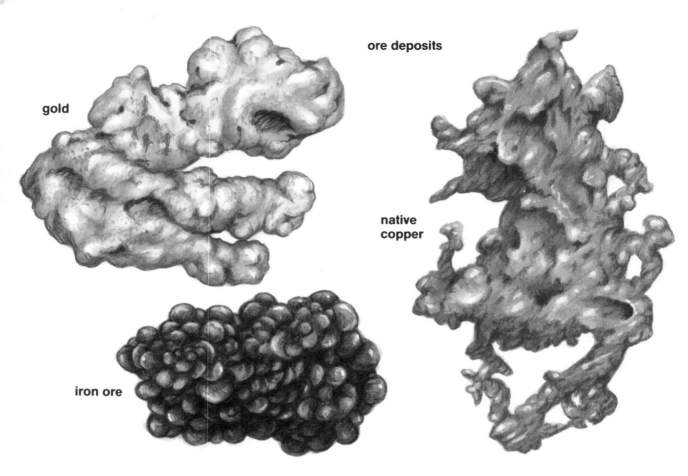

gold

ore deposits

native
copper

iron ore

Ore—Worth Its Weight

Some rocks contain useful minerals—such metals as iron, lead, gold, silver, copper, and other valuable substances. When a substance can be taken out of the rock and then used, the rock is called an *ore*. Copper ore is a rock that contains enough copper minerals to make it valuable.

Sometimes it costs too much or is too difficult to take the metal from the rock. In these cases, the rock is not called ore. To be called ore, it must make money for the people who separate the substance from the rocks.

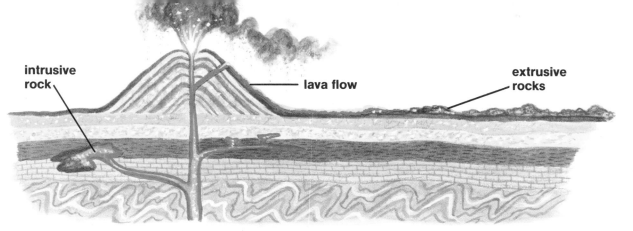

intrusive rock

lava flow

extrusive rocks

The Oldest Rocks

The world's oldest rocks were formed many millions of years ago. Made of cooled, hardened magma, they are called **igneous rocks**. Igneous rocks are made up of two groups: *extrusive* and *intrusive*. Extrusive rocks are formed when magma erupts from volcanoes and flows onto the surface, where it cools. Intrusive rocks are formed when magma cools beneath the earth's surface.

Basalt

Three types of extrusive rock are **basalt, obsidian,** and **pumice**. Basalt is a dark, heavy rock and the most common of all lava rocks. The Hawaiian islands are almost completely basalt.

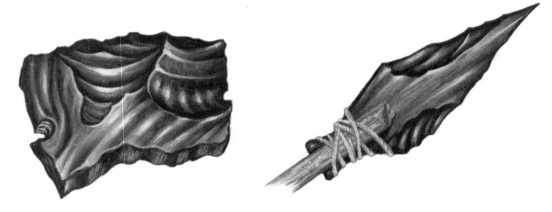

Obsidian

Obsidian, a natural glass, is a shiny black rock. Because it breaks into pieces with sharp edges, obsidian was used by primitive people for spearheads, arrowheads, digging tools, jewelry, and other items.

Pumice

Pumice is a foamy rock made up of many glass threads. It is light gray and filled with pockets of air. Pumice is so light in weight that it floats on water. It is also called feather rock. Ground into a powder, pumice is used for cleaning, smoothing, and polishing.

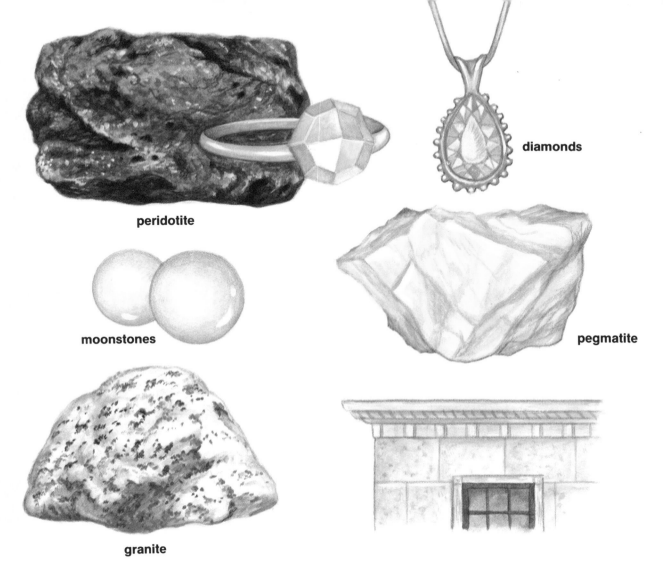

diamonds

peridotite

moonstones

pegmatite

granite

Rocks Can Be Gems

Intrusive igneous rocks are often the source of fine gems. **Peridotite,** for example, can have diamonds in it. **Pegmatite** can contain moonstones and other gems. The most common intrusive rock is **granite**. Usually light in color, granite is widely used in buildings and for monuments.

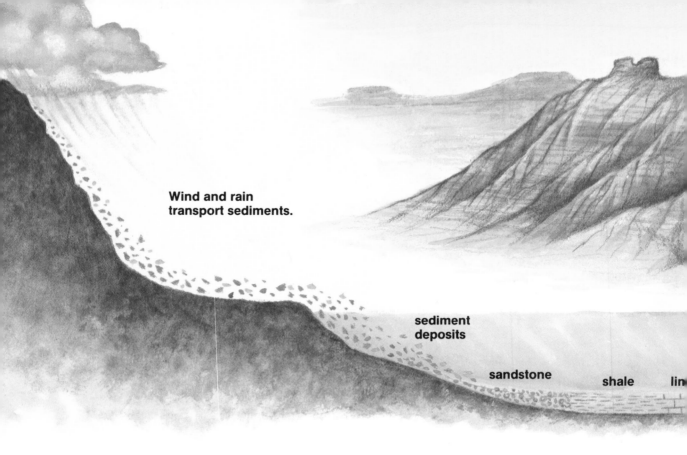

Wind and rain transport sediments.

sediment deposits

sandstone

shale

lin

Sedimentary Rock

Every time a bit of rock erodes, it is carried to some other place. Wind or water will drop it on the ground, in a lake or ocean...anywhere. These bits of rock are called **sediment**.

As centuries go by, these layers of sediment grow thicker and higher. In time, the layers harden and become **sedimentary rock**. Two kinds of sedimentary rock are formed, depending on whether the layers were made of rock moved in bits and pieces, or rock that had been dissolved in water.

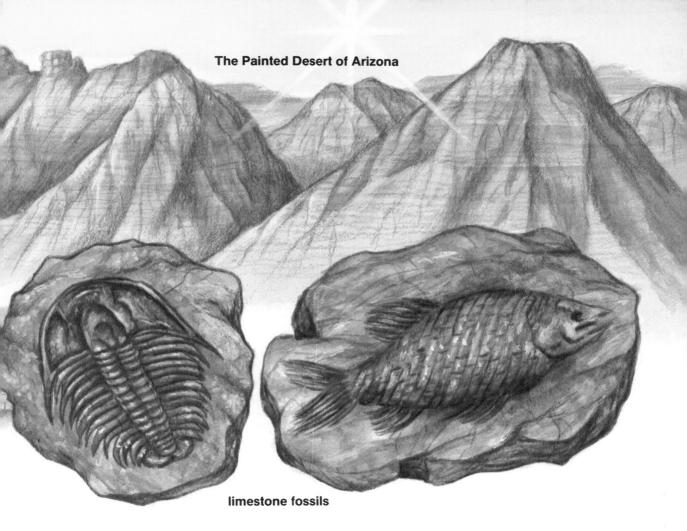

The Painted Desert of Arizona

limestone fossils

Sedimentary rocks can be hard or soft. They can be all colors. The famous Painted Desert of Arizona is a perfect example of the wide color range of sedimentary rock.

If you pick up a rock that has layers, you are holding a piece of sedimentary rock. If the rock has fossils in it, you are probably holding a piece of **limestone**. Fossils are the remains or the marks made by animals or plants that lived many thousands or millions of years ago.

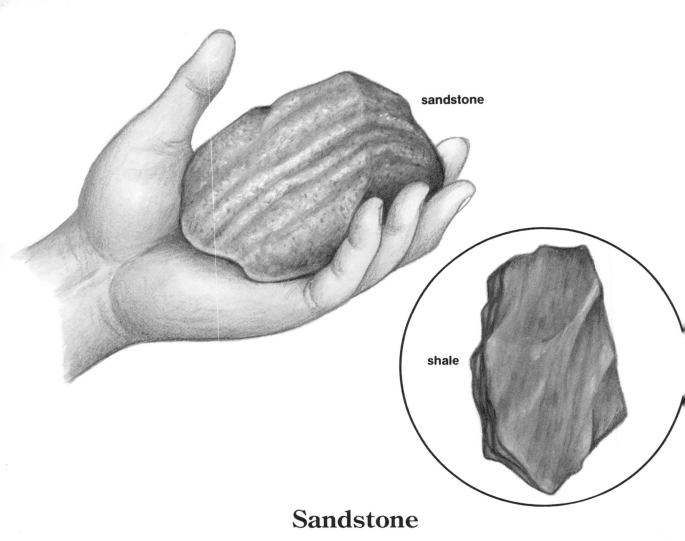

sandstone

shale

Sandstone

If the rock you pick up is made mostly of sand, and is red, brown, gray, yellow, or white, you have found a piece of **sandstone**. Sandstone is made of the mineral called *quartz*. Sometimes the piece of sandstone has a stripe running through it. This band is made by other kinds of minerals.

If your next find is a rock that is relatively soft, breaks easily, and is gray, or black, or dull red, you have some **shale**. Shale is made of mud and clay. It is used in making bricks and cement.

Coal

Limestone is not the only kind of rock that contains fossils. Some **coal** often has signs of the ferns and other plants that grew where the coal began to form. These plants were living in very swampy land. As the plants died, they fell into the swamps. Over centuries, mud and plants built up, one layer on top of another. With the addition of new layers, pressure increased on the bottom layers. This pushed the water and gases out of them. What was left was a dark material called *carbon*. Coal is solid carbon.

**coal containing
fern fossil**

There are two kinds of coal. Coal that still has some gas and water in it is called *bituminous* or *soft coal*. Soft coal is the kind used in stoves and furnaces today.

Coal with no gas or water in it is called *anthracite* or *hard coal*, which is expensive and used primarily in high-temperature furnaces. You are not likely to find any traces of fossils in hard coal.

Dolomite

Rock in different forms is often used for buildings. One kind that is found and used throughout the world is called **dolomite**. Dolomite is pink or white. Remember limestone? Well, dolomite is limestone that changed when a silver-white element called *magnesium* replaced some of the calcium in limestone.

Dolomite may also form on the inside of *geodes*. Geodes are round stones, often shaped like baseballs or footballs. They have rough surfaces, but their rough outside hides a beautiful inside. Break open a geode and you will find a treasure of dolomite and other minerals, typically as glittery, colorful crystals!

geode

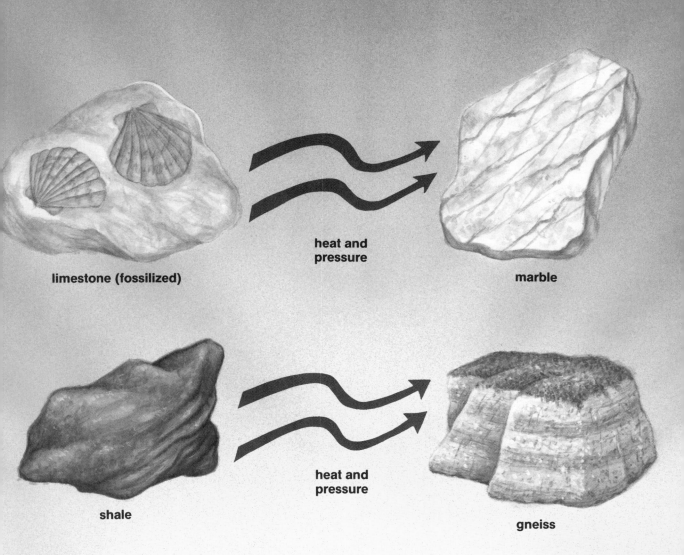

limestone (fossilized) — heat and pressure → marble

shale — heat and pressure → gneiss

Metamorphic Rock

Now you know about igneous and sedimentary rock. There is a third kind—**metamorphic rock**. Metamorphic rock means "rock that has changed." How? Nature squeezed the rock, bent it, heated it, stretched it, or did something else that changed the rock from one form to another.

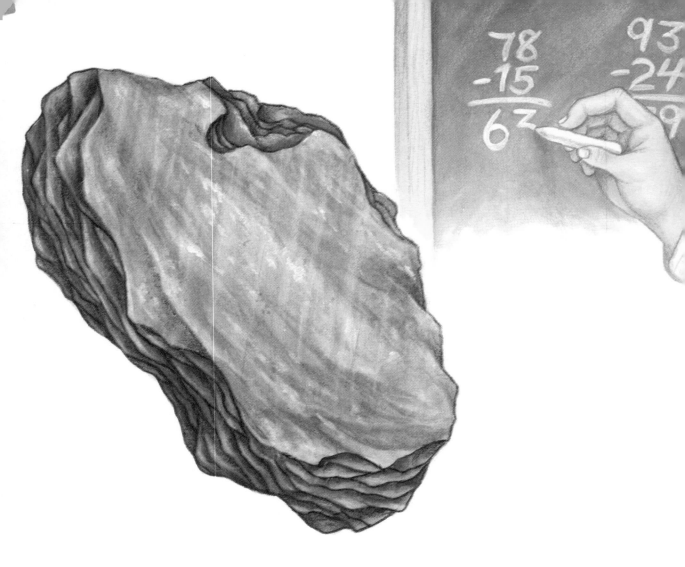

Slate

Slate is a fine-grained metamorphic rock. Before it became slate, it was the soft sedimentary rock called shale. Heat and pressure metamorphized—changed—soft shale into hard slate. Teachers and athletic coaches write on slate boards with chalk.

Marble

Marble is another kind of metamorphic rock. Marble was once limestone. As heat and pressure turned it into a hard rock, shale and other rocks were twisted inside the limestone. All this created beautiful dark streaks running through the marble. Polished marble is used for statues, monuments, and buildings. Many people think marble is the most beautiful of all the rocks.

Schist

A close "cousin" of marble and slate is **schist** (to rhyme with
twist). Schist is formed mostly of *mica* that is made of different
kinds of minerals and is flaky and bendable. Schist can easily
be split or divided into layers. In fact, the name schist comes
from a Greek word that means "to divide." Because mica comes
in different colors, schist does, too. It can be silvery, red, black,
green—nearly every color imaginable.

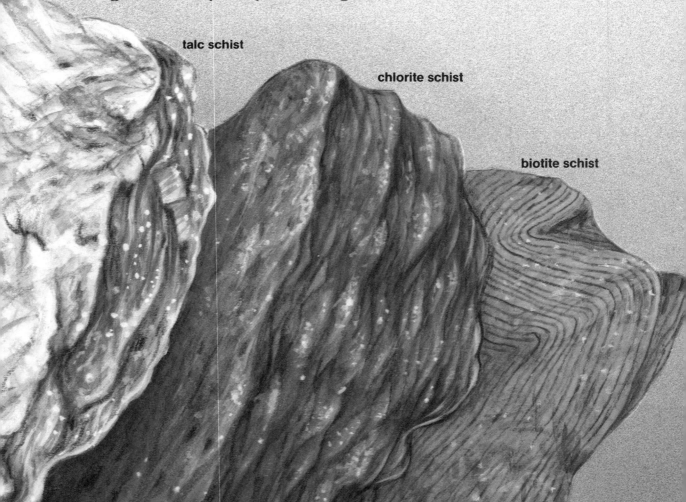

talc schist

chlorite schist

biotite schist

Gneiss

Another metamorphic rock is called **gneiss** (said just like "nice"). And it comes in some very nice colors, such as green, pink, gray, and white.

Gneiss is not one kind of rock. It is any metamorphic rock with dark-colored and light-colored bands next to each other. These bands are made of different kinds of minerals. The color of the gneiss is determined by its mineral content.

Collecting

So now you know that rocks come in different colors, sizes, shapes, and degrees of hardness. And that you can find them everywhere. You are ready to start your own rock collection. A rock collection can provide an interesting subject for a school report. It can earn you a merit badge in scouting. But most important, it will reward you with fun, excitement, and discovery for the rest of your life. It starts with a pebble here...a stone there...